Helping Children See Jesus

ISBN: 978-1-933206-95-0

The Walking Umbrella Antonio of Brazil

Author: Rose-Mae Carvin
Illustrator: Frances H. Hertzler
Typesetting and Layout: Morgan Melton, Patricia Pope

© 2018 Bible Visuals International
PO Box 153, Akron, PA 17501-0153
Phone: (717) 859-1131
www.biblevisuals.org

All rights reserved. No part of this publication may be reproduced, stored in a retrieval system or transmitted in any form by any means, electronic, mechanical, photocopy, recording or otherwise, without the prior permission of the publisher, except as provided by USA copyright law.

RELATED ITEMS

To access related items (such as activities, memory verse posters and translated texts) please visit our web store at shop.biblevisuals.org and enter 5585 in the search box on the page.

FREE TEXT DOWNLOAD

To access a FREE printable copy of the teaching text (PDF format) in English or other available languages, enter S5585DL in the search box. Add the item to your cart, and use coupon code XTACSV17 at checkout. Once your order is processed you will receive an email with a link to the free download.

For God so loved the world, that He gave His only begotten Son, that WHOSOEVER believeth in Him should not perish, but have everlasting life.

John 3:16

Go, go, go, go!
the Bible says to go
To ev'ry land,
till ev'ry man
and boy and girl
shall know

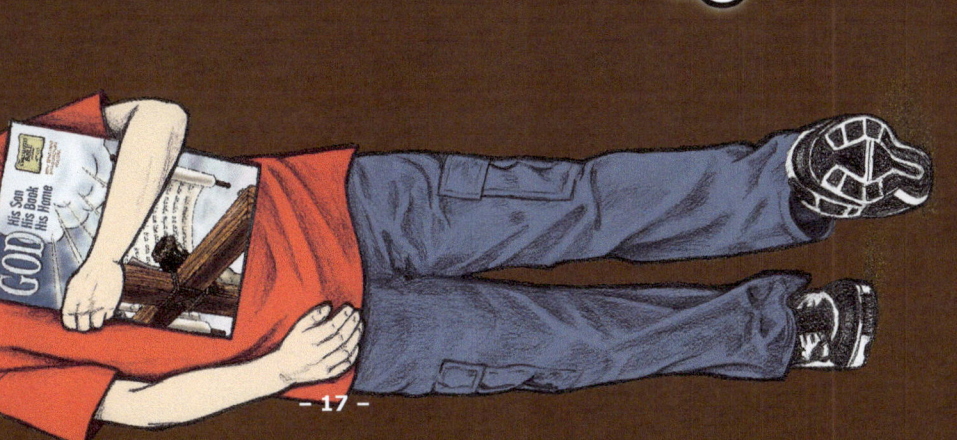

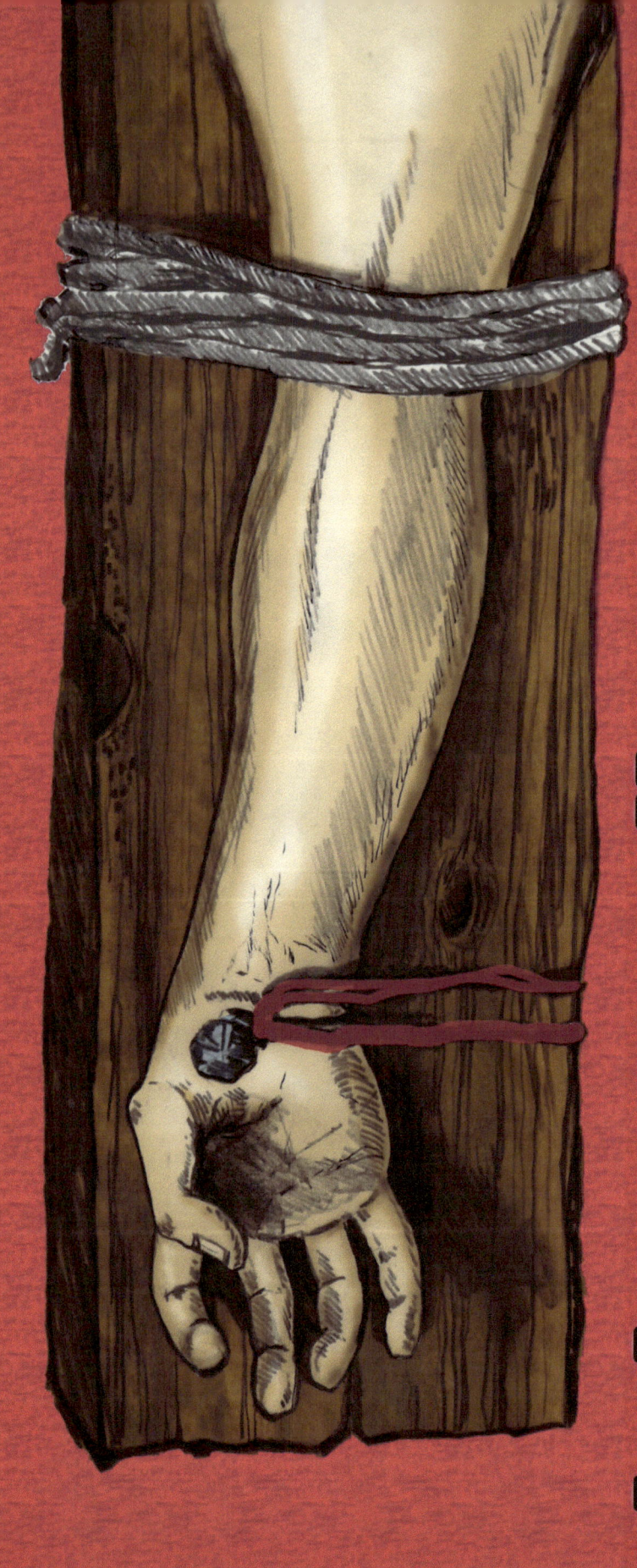

That Jesus died on Calv'ry's tree to bring to all salvation free.

Oh, who who will go? Oh, will Oh, will YOU go?

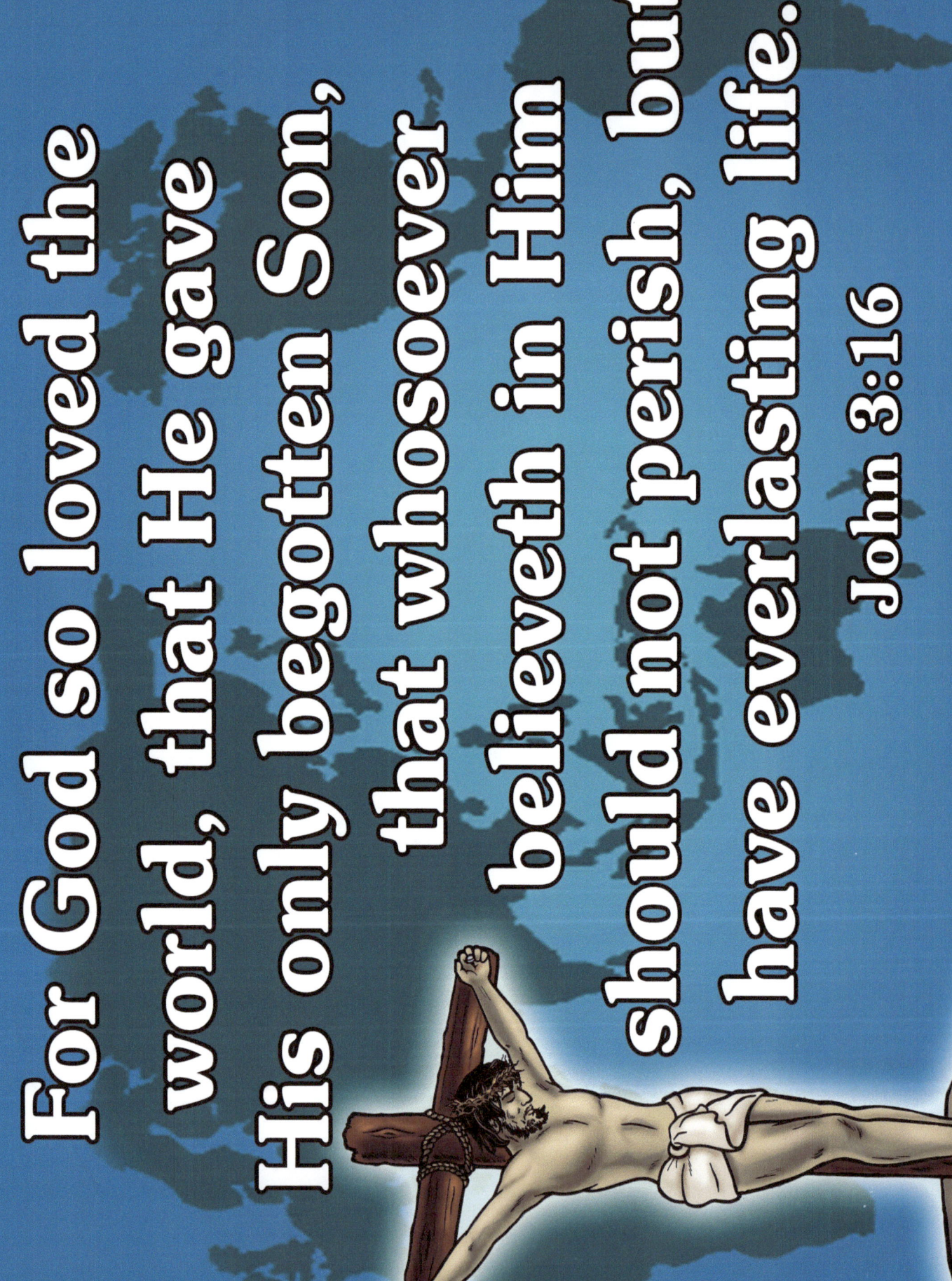

The Walking Umbrella

Would you like to hear about a walking umbrella? If you had been in Wilmington, Delaware, you could have seen it with your own eyes, for it really, truly happened.

Show Illustration #1

A big, big umbrella was moving quickly down the street. It seemed to be walking by itself, low to the ground. It was a beautiful, bright, many-colored umbrella. Man-sized, it bobbed, bobbed, bobbed along.

Show Illustration #2

Everyone was curious about the strange umbrella. So boys and girls and grown-ups followed it. Soon they discovered that the small feet which carried the umbrella belonged to a nice black boy. He walked quietly and quickly. The watchers followed.

Finally he came to a shady spot under a huge tree. He put the big umbrella on the ground.

Show Illustration #3

"Who wants to hear the story about my umbrella?" he asked. The children crowded close to him. "Sit down and listen," he ordered. Everyone obeyed, even though some of his listeners were larger than he.

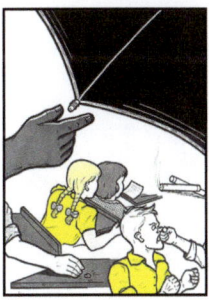

Show Illustration #4

He pointed to the part of his umbrella that was colored black. "See this black color?" he began. "Black makes us think of sin and of darkness. Every one of us has done something wrong at some time or other. Usually we do wrong things when no one is around. Or we do them in the dark when no one can see us. The wrong things we do are sin." Everyone listened closely.

Show Illustration #5

"Now see this gold color? That makes us think of heaven, where the street is made of gold. No sin can ever get inside heaven. If it did, it would spoil heaven. There is no sin there. So none of us can go to heaven because all of us do wrong, sinful things." The listeners were sad.

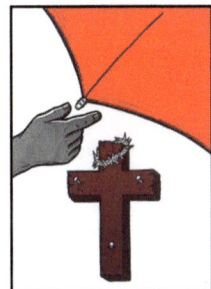

Show Illustration #6

"But see this red color?" he continued. "This tells us that the Lord Jesus Christ died on the cross and shed His precious blood to forgive our sins. The Lord Jesus is the Son of God. He took the punishment we deserve. When we believe that He is God's Son and receive Him as our Saviour, He forgives our sin and…

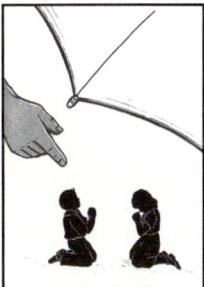

Show Illustration #7

…makes our hearts clean and pure, like this white color in my umbrella. But we have to believe Him. We have to trust Him. We have to ask Him to forgive our sins. When we do, He comes into our lives and becomes our Saviour! He gives us His kind of life–everlasting life. He sees to it that we can go to heaven when we die."

Show Illustration #8

He continued, "How many of you know that you are sinners but you want to go to heaven some day?" Up went every hand. "All right then, tell God you are a sinner."

Quickly and quietly the children knelt on the ground. Each spoke reverently to God, confessing his sin. "Now tell Him you believe the Lord Jesus Christ is God's Son and that He died for you. Ask Him to forgive your sins and save you right now, for Jesus' sake." Softly the children prayed.

Show Illustration #9

The boy then took a small Bible (a New Testament) out of his pocket. He opened to the third chapter of John, verse sixteen. "Now I am going to read a verse from God's Holy Word. When I come to the words 'the world,' you must put your name there instead. Then when I come to the word 'whosoever,' you put your name instead. Do you understand? 'For God so loved *the world* (John Doe), that He gave His only begotten Son, that *whosoever* (John Doe, who) believeth in Him should not perish, but have everlasting life.'"

Each one read the verse and substituted his own name. "This means that if you have believed that God loves you, if you really, truly believe that He sent His Son to die for you, and if you have honestly believed in the Lord Jesus Christ and received Him into your heart, you are born into God's family, And all who are in God's family have everlasting life. This is God's Word. And it is absolutely true." He paused a moment.

Show Illustration #10

"But I have another color in this umbrella. What color did I leave out?"

His listeners chorused, "Green!"

"That's right. I did not tell you about the green. Well, it's like this. After we receive the Lord Jesus and are made ready for heaven by His precious blood. He expects us to grow to be better and better Christians every day. The green makes us think of growing things–like green trees and grass. You won't grow to be a strong Christian unless you read your Bible and pray every day, and go to Sunday school. Now don't forget this."

He closed his umbrella. "Now I want you all to run off and tell somebody else the things I have told you. I'll come back here tomorrow and see how many of you can tell me what I have told you about the colors.

*Everybody that can tell me what they mean, and how to get saved, will get a little book with these colors in it, so you can tell it to someone else."

The children did run off in every direction. At once, they told others what they had done. And the boy started down the street, his umbrella open again, to get another group to whom he could tell the Gospel.

You know, what the boy told his followers is true. (Teacher will repeat the Gospel using the Wordless Book colors, pointing to the different pages in this book.)

And just as the children there in Delaware received the Lord Jesus Christ as Saviour, you may do so, too, right this very minute. (*Teacher:* Give a clear and definite invitation, concluding with prayer. Be certain to use John 3:16 as he did. And by all means, encourage them to witness to someone else.)

*Do not tell this part of the story, unless you plan to do the same with children to whom you are witnessing.

Used by permission of Union Gospel Press

Based on a true event
Antonio of Brazil

Show Illustration #11

"Dona Sylvina, may I come to the Bible Class you have here in our school?"

It was a little Brazilian boy–speaking Portuguese! In Brazil, South America, the national language is Portuguese.

"Of course, Antonio, if your parents give their permission. Take this letter home with you. If they sign it giving their permission, you may surely come to all the classes."

"Thank you, Dona, thank you very much." Antonio hoped his parents would sign the letter, for he wanted to study the Bible. Dona Sylvina prayed each day for the boy, and that his parents would give their permission.

Show Illustration #12

The very next week, Antonio came rushing into the class with a happy smile, he waved the letter in his hand. "It is signed," he said. "See Dona Sylvina? It is signed!"

Antonio was so excited that he sat on the edge of his chair listening to the teacher as she taught. In his heart there was a longing to know about the things of God–a longing God puts into the hearts of boys and girls everywhere. Often they do not know *what* they want–but they know they yearn for *something*–something which will help them to know God.

Show Illustration #13

Antonio was amazed as the teacher told that God had sent His Son the Lord Jesus Christ, to earth and that the Lord Jesus *wanted* to die for the sins of everyone. And, because He is God the Son, he arose from the dead. The teacher explained, "Those who receive Him can be free of punishment for sin and will some day go to heaven to live with Him forever."

"Poh!" he said (which is what boys in Brazil say when they mean "Wow!"). "They couldn't keep *Him* in a grave! He got right out and left His burial clothes in the tomb. Poh!"

Antonio did not realize he was talking out loud. But when he saw the teacher looking at him, he slid down in his chair embarrassed. Boys and girls in Brazil do not talk out loud in class, unless they are asked to do so.

This was what Antonio had been longing for, deep in his heart. When the teacher invited the boys and girls to accept the Lord Jesus as *their* Saviour, he was the first to receive Him.

Show Illustration #14

"Now I'll come to class every week," he said, "because now *I am a Christian*." He smiled happily as he said again, "Poh!"

Antonio not only came to the school's Bible class every week, but he began going to a Sunday school. He knew many of the songs because they were the same songs they sang in class. He lifted his voice and sang with all his heart. And he never missed the Bible class at school.

Show Illustration #15

"Where can I get some of the pictures and things you use, Dona?" he asked one day. "I want to start a Bible class at home and try to teach some of my cousins and playmates."

"If you will be very careful of them, I shall lend you some of mine," the teacher said.

Antonio began right away. There were three children at his first class, but more kept coming. One week there were 11 who sat and listened to the Bible lessons and Gospel stories Antonio told.

Show Illustration #16

One of the stories was *The Walking Umbrella*. When he returned it to the teacher she said, "Antonio, would you like to tell this story to the class today?" Delighted Antonio began!

"See," he said, "this boy who lives in the United States (and this is a true story!) took this big umbrella made of all these colors and went walking along the streets. Boys and girls followed him. When he thought there were enough, he stopped. He made them sit down on the ground. Then he told the children how they could be saved using the colors to remind them of the darkness of sin (the black); of Jesus' blood shed on the cross to forgive sin (red); of clean hearts after accepting the Lord Jesus as Saviour (white); and how Christians should grow to be better and better every day, as the grass and trees grow" (green).

When he finished telling the story, Antonio added, "If you'd like to become Christians, or even if you think you are one, how about saying John 3:16 after me? You say your own name wherever the verse says 'the world,' or 'whosoever'." Antonio explained, "Do it like this: 'For God so loved ANTONIO that He gave His only begotten Son, that ANTONIO who believes in Him, should not perish, but have everlasting life.'"

Afterwards, Antonio said to Dona Sylvina. "Poh! I don't have to wait until I'm big to be a missionary, do I? Only, of course, after I've grown up and studied the Bible n' everything, I'll be able to do better. Poh!"

Antonio's black eyes flashed. They were filled with excitement and happiness. His big smile seemed to cover most of his tanned face. Antonio of Brazil is a missionary indeed!

Be a Missionary

J. IRVIN OVERHOLTZER
WENDELL P. LOVELESS

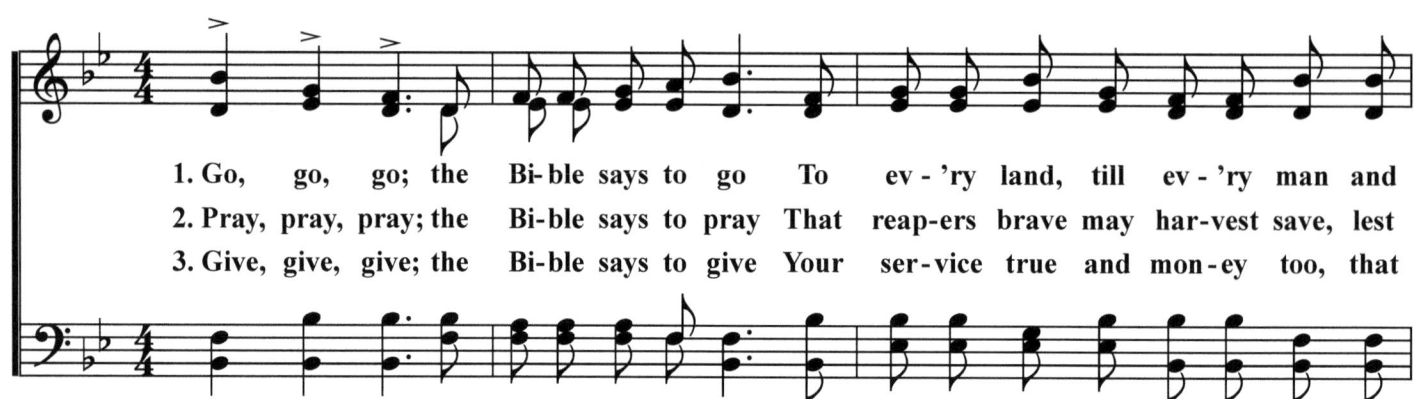

1. Go, go, go; the Bi-ble says to go To ev-'ry land, till ev-'ry man and
2. Pray, pray, pray; the Bi-ble says to pray That reap-ers brave may har-vest save, lest
3. Give, give, give; the Bi-ble says to give Your ser-vice true and mon-ey too, that

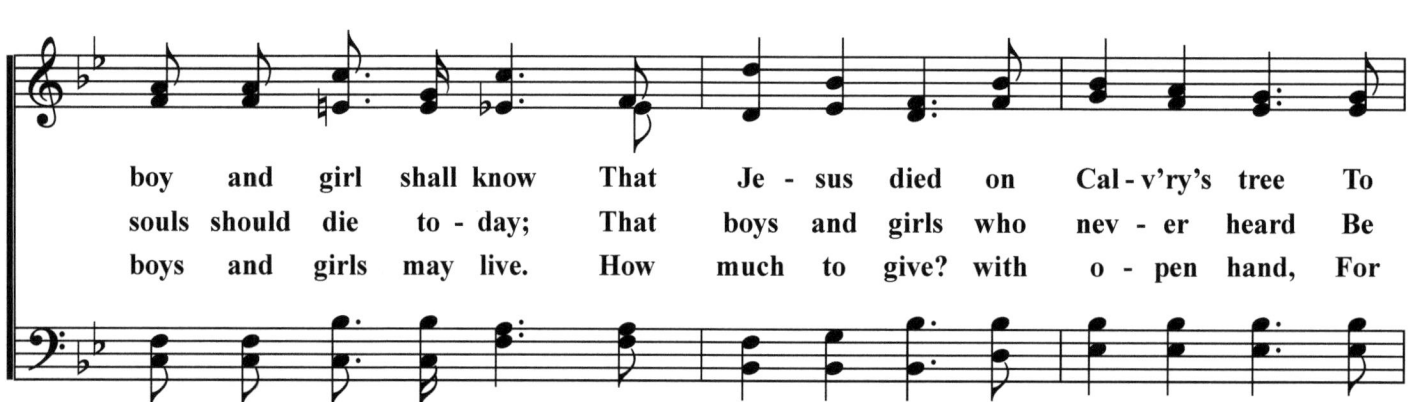

boy and girl shall know That Je - sus died on Cal - v'ry's tree To
souls should die to - day; That boys and girls who nev - er heard Be
boys and girls may live. How much to give? with o - pen hand, For

bring to all sal - va - tion free. Oh, who will go? Oh, will you go?
plain - ly told the bless - ed Word. Oh, who will pray? Oh, will you pray?
Je - sus' sake give all you can. Oh, who will give? Oh, will you give?

Copyright 1938. Renewal 1966 by Ruth P. Overholtzer in Salvation Songs #1
Assigned to Child Evangelism Fellowship, Inc. All rights reserved. Used by permission.
Permission is granted to make one copy of this sheet music for your pianist.

www.ingramcontent.com/pod-product-compliance
Lightning Source LLC
Chambersburg PA
CBHW060807090426
42736CB00002B/194